P9-DCZ-699

RACIAL PROFILING

Essential Viewpoints

RACIAL PROFILING

BY TAMRA ORR

Content Consultant
Eric W. Mogren, JD, PhD
Associate Professor, History
Northern Illinois University

ABDO
Publishing Company

CREDITS

Published by ABDO Publishing Company, 8000 West 78th Street, Edina, Minnesota 55439. Copyright © 2010 by Abdo Consulting Group, Inc. International copyrights reserved in all countries. No part of this book may be reproduced in any form without written permission from the publisher. The Essential Library™ is a trademark and logo of ABDO Publishing Company.

Printed in the United States.

Editor: Amy Van Zee
Copy Editor: Paula Lewis
Interior Design and Production: Emily Love
Cover Design: Emily Love

Library of Congress Cataloging-in-Publication Data
Orr, Tamra.
 Racial profiling / by Tamra Orr.
    p. cm. — (Essential viewpoints)
 Includes bibliographical references and index.
 ISBN 978-1-60453-535-8
 1. Racial profiling in law enforcement—United States—Juvenile literature. I. Title.
 HV8141.O75 2009
 363.2'308900973—dc22

                         2008034915

TABLE OF CONTENTS

Many instances of racial profiling occur at airports.

At the Airport

You have just spent the holidays with your family and are at the airport to return home. You make your way to your gate, show your boarding pass, board the plane, make a quick trip to the restroom, and then settle into your seat. Before long, your eyes become heavy and, ignoring the rather boisterous passengers seated next to you, you tilt your head back and drift to sleep. Suddenly, you are jolted awake and are escorted from the plane without any explanation.

For Portuguese-born U.S. citizen John Cerqueira, this was stark reality. On December 28, 2003, Cerqueira, a computer consultant who spent a great deal of time traveling the country, was removed from an American Airlines flight from Boston, Massachusetts, to Florida. The two Israeli men sitting next to him were taken off the flight as well. They were not told why.

A Story of Seatmates

Cerqueira was puzzled. Cerqueira, along with the two Israeli men who had been sitting next to him, was interrogated for two hours. "There were a lot of questions as to how I knew the other two, how the other two knew me, what we were all doing on the plane," he says. "But we weren't given any information. We were detained and just asked questions."[1]

At the end of the questioning, Cerqueira and the other two men were taken to an American Airlines counter and told they were "released for travel," although they were not allowed to book a ticket on any other American Airlines plane. Cerqueira was unnerved by the incident and decided to pursue his legal options.

A LEGAL MATTER

John Cerqueira filed a lawsuit against American Airlines for the racial profiling they had used when removing him from the plane. He contended that the airline had decided he was of Arab or Middle Eastern descent and that was enough to make him a security threat. Following a six-day trial, the Boston, Massachusetts, jury agreed with Cerqueira. On January 15, 2007, they awarded him $400,000. His case is considered the first official legal victory in airline racial profiling after the terrorist events of 9/11.

But after the case was heard, American Airlines appealed the decision. On January 10, 2008, the U.S. Court of Appeals vacated the lower court's decision because the lower court failed to inform the jury of the airline's right to remove passengers under law. This case represents one aspect in the conflict over racial profiling: Do airlines have the right to take an action, in the name of safety, that could potentially infringe upon one's civil rights? On January 24, 2008, Cerqueira's attorneys filed a petition for a rehearing.

During a radio interview with a daily news program called *Democracy Now!*, Michael Kirkpatrick, Cerqueira's attorney, asserted,

> *Our theory was that if Mr. Cerqueira did not have a Middle Eastern appearance, if he wasn't perceived to be Middle Eastern, and if hadn't been sitting next to these other two gentlemen who were from the Middle East, and they were speaking in a foreign language, none of this ever would have happened. And that's racial profiling. That's discrimination, and it's against the law.* [2]

Cerqueira discussed what happened with news media because he hoped the situation would be spread to the public. He ultimately wants his story to stop future acts of racial profiling.

From the Other Side

After the Boston jury's verdict in Cerqueira's case, American Airlines sent the following statement to the press: "While we respect the jury system, we disagree with this verdict. This decision is simply not supported by the facts or the law. We will evaluate our legal options." In response, Cerqueira says, "I'm dismayed and discouraged that to this day they disagree that something that they did was wrong." [3]

The Heart of the Controversy

Cerqueira's question goes right to the core of the issue of racial profiling. Racial profiling means using race as a determining factor in taking steps to prevent crime and in determining whom to investigate. Is a person more likely to be a criminal based on the color of his or her skin? Is it right for law enforcement officers, especially in airports, to take race or ethnicity into account when determining whom to investigate, interrogate, or search? Many assume the United States left these beliefs behind with the issues of slavery, the Civil

Dangerous Derbies?

Sandra Rana is a member of the Tulsa Police Community Race Relations Committee. She was at a Texas airport wearing her hijab, the traditional head covering of Muslim women, when airport officials targeted her and her eight-year-old son Omar. Omar was holding something important to him—the Boy Scout pinewood derby car he had recently built. The officials not only took it away from him but also began tearing it apart. Rana said, "Imagine how I felt when my eight-year-old son was pulled from the line because of his name and I could not go with him. Imagine how he felt when they started to take apart his Boy Scout pinewood derby car. . . . It is now routine for my son . . . to get extra security checks at the airport. He knows it's going to happen, and he expects it. . . . But how do I tell my . . . son that it's okay? He is now ten. He is learning about civil liberties and civil rights. What meaning do they have for him . . . ?" Since then, Rana does not wear her hijab and reminds her children not to speak Urdu or bring along the Quran. Her best advice now is "Don't do anything that will cause attention to yourself."[4]

War, and the civil rights movement. But according to statistics, racial discrimination remains prevalent throughout the nation today. For example, a 2005 report by the American Civil Liberties Union (ACLU) showed that minority drivers in Rhode Island were more than twice as likely as white drivers to be searched during traffic stops.

A HOUSE STUDY

In June of 2000, the Minnesota House of Representatives released a report detailing the issues and methodology of racial profiling in law enforcement. The report says that minority members perceive that racial profiling is widespread, while officers in law enforcement agencies deny that it is occurring. The officers say that law enforcement focuses on behavioral and other indicators when determining whom to investigate, not only race. Prior

A Primary Definition

Section 3 of Bill S2481, the End Racial Profiling Act, prohibits racial profiling, which is defined as "the practice of a law enforcement agent relying, to any degree, on race, ethnicity, national origin or religion in selecting which individuals to subject to routine or spontaneous investigatory activities or in deciding upon the scope and substance of law enforcement activity following the initial investigatory procedure, except when there is trustworthy information, relevant to the locality and timeframe, that links a person of a particular race, ethnicity, national origin or religion to an identified criminal incident or scheme."[5]

to 9/11, those who argued in favor of racial profiling said that it should be used in combination with other factors, such as age, dress, time of day, and location. Those against racial profiling said that it violates constitutional rights, no matter how it is used.

In June 2001, Congress authored a bill to end racial profiling. Civil rights groups and law enforcement agencies held meetings and provided educational training to put a stop to the practice of racial profiling.

Terrorism

Perhaps progress was being made, but all of that changed with the horrific events of September 11, 2001. Suddenly, the people of the United States looked at racial profiling through a completely different lens. The 19 hijackers of the airliners were men of Middle Eastern descent with connections to the

Ashcroft's Words

At a Senate Judiciary Committee Hearing on November 6, 2001, Attorney General John Ashcroft stated, "To those who pit Americans against immigrants, citizens against non-citizens, to those who scare peace-loving people with phantoms of lost liberty, my message is this: Your tactics only aid terrorists for they erode our national unity and diminish our resolve. . . . They give ammunition to America's enemies and pause to America's friends. They encourage people of good will to remain silent in the face of evil. Our efforts have been crafted carefully to avoid infringing on constitutional rights, while saving American lives."[6]

Edgardo Cureg, left, was taken off a Continental Airlines flight because other passengers said they "felt uncomfortable" traveling with him.

terrorist organization al-Qaeda. With these men at the helm of the largest terrorist act in U.S. history, it did not take long for many Americans to look at all dark-skinned foreigners with suspicion and fear. Today, the debate centers on the use of racial profiling as a determining factor in the prevention of terrorism.

A Heated Issue

The events of 9/11 greatly complicated the issue of racial profiling in the United States. Because the 9/11 terrorists had similar racial backgrounds, some people have begun to believe that racial profiling is necessary in order to prevent another attack on U.S. soil. Some people believe that stopping terror and crime is worth the inconvenience of creating unpleasant circumstances for the accused. They believe that political correctness puts the lives of U.S. citizens at risk. Political correctness is the effort to implement societal changes that make amends for past injustices against people of a certain race, gender, or religion. Political correctness aims to use language and policies that do not offend anyone. But those who are in favor of racial profiling say that politically correct actions are dangerous because they place personal rights above national security.

People who argue in favor of racial profiling, however, face accusations of discrimination and racism. They are also accused of violating the civil liberties protected by the U.S. Constitution. Because of this, it can be difficult to find outspoken proponents of racial profiling. The proponents who are vocal claim that, although few admit to it, many people silently agree with the concept of using racial profiling to avoid terrorist attacks.

Opponents of racial profiling say not only is it a flawed concept, but that those who use it are wrong far more often than they are right. These people contend that racial profiling is a gross violation of privacy and personal rights, and racial profiling should not be used. There are many personal stories of minority members being detained or interrogated because of the color of their skin. U.S. history has provided many examples of racism and prejudice against minorities. With all of the progress made toward racial harmony in the United States, opponents

Consolation

If racial profiling is to be used in airports, some have suggested that the innocent who are profiled should receive consolation for being singled out. In cases where people have been removed from airplanes, some of these people are given boarding passes on different planes to continue their travel.

of racial profiling fear that the practice of racial profiling will undo the progress the United States has worked to achieve.

Is racial profiling a necessary part of protecting the people of the United States? Is it a breach of every person's civil rights? The debate continues with passion and reason on both sides. ⌐

The Transportation Security Administration was formed soon after 9/11.

An artistic rendering of the discovery of the slave Nat Turner after his rebellion against his white owner

A LOOK BACK
THROUGH HISTORY

lthough the targets of racial profiling have changed throughout U.S. history, the practice has remained much the same. U.S. citizens have previously placed blame on specific racial groups and acted in racist manners. Racism is a belief that race determines behavior, and racism usually incorporates a mind-set that one race is better than another.

Because the practice of racial profiling makes assumptions about people based on their appearance, opponents say that racial profiling cannot be separated from racism. Throughout its history, the United States has battled racism. Its people have fought to create a nation that gives equal opportunity to all. Does the practice of racial profiling negate that progress?

THE AGE OF SLAVERY

Racism was practiced in the United States when African Americans were kept as slaves. In 1669, the Commonwealth of Virginia passed the Casual Slave Killing Act. It gave blanket permission to owners to kill their slaves if they thought it was best. To slave owners, their slaves were their property, which meant they could do what they liked with them. This often meant mistreatment, and in some cases, death.

The mistreatment of African Americans continued. In 1831, Virginia slave Nat Turner led a small rebellion to free slaves and kill white people. In retaliation for the death of almost 60 whites in

Nat Turner's Rebellion, more than 250 blacks were captured and killed by the government and private citizens. Whether the African Americans were part of the massacre was irrelevant. Their skin was black, so they were killed.

CIVIL LIBERTIES

In 1868, the states ratified the Fourteenth Amendment, which provided legal protection for U.S. citizens. It also declared that states could not deprive a citizen of life and liberty. This amendment provides for civil liberties. But as time went on and the United States faced international crises, these civil

Lasting Words

In 1953, Earl Warren became the fourteenth chief justice of the United States. For many Americans, he was a spokesperson for their beliefs in the importance of maintaining civil rights and protecting personal freedom. Early in his career, Warren served as the attorney general of California and spoke out against prejudice based on national origin. His words are just as significant and meaningful today. In 1940, he stated,

It should be remembered that practically all aliens have come to this country because they like our land and our institutions better than those from whence they came. They have attached themselves to the life of this country in a manner that they would hate to change and the vast majority of them will, if given a chance, remain the same good neighbors that they have been in the past regardless of what difficulties our nation may have with the country of their birth. History proves this to be true. . . . We must see to it that no race prejudices develop and that there are no petty persecutions of law-abiding people.[1]

liberties were not always upheld
and enforced to their fullest extent.
Times of war have historically led
to racist actions, even by those in
government office.

A Country at War

One element that changes the
emphasis on racial profiling is war,
or the threat of it. When a country
is at war, the country can create a
sharper, more focused image of the
enemy—and often, innocent people
are included in this image. The
United States became embroiled in

"All persons born or naturalized in the United States, and subject to the jurisdiction thereof, are citizens of the United States and of the State wherein they reside. No State shall make or enforce any law which shall abridge the privileges of immunities of citizens of the United States; nor shall any State deprive any person of life, liberty, or property, without due process of the law; nor deny to any person within its jurisdiction the equal protection of the laws."[2]

—*Amendment Fourteen,
Section One*

such incidents of racial profiling. Events from World
War I and World War II carried on into the War on
Terror. Once again, racial profiling would emerge
from the shadows and into newspaper headlines.

After World War I (1914–1918) ended, the
nation endured many internal struggles. While the
battles had ended on the war front, many battles
continued on the home front. Prices on goods and
commodities were rising, and nationwide strikes
were common. In 1917, the Eighteenth Amendment

made alcohol illegal. In 1920, women were given the right to vote by the Nineteenth Amendment. There were many changes occurring within the United States during the first few decades of the twentieth century.

The war was over, but people had something new to fear: the "Red Scare." Many feared that communists would take over the United States. When a series of bombings occurred during the summer of 1919 that were blamed on Americans of German and Russian heritage, people grew even more frightened. The bombs targeted some of the nation's most important cities, including Washington DC. One of the homes partially destroyed by a bomb belonged to U.S. Attorney General A. Mitchell Palmer.

THE PALMER RAIDS

Palmer understood that President Woodrow Wilson was involved with the Treaty of Versailles, the peace treaty that ended World War I. Wilson was also occupied with health problems and other pressing matters. Still, Palmer was concerned about the potential threat radical immigrant groups posed to the country. He called these people "hyphenated Americans." He formed the General Intelligence

Attorney General A. Mitchell Palmer believed that communism was a large threat to the United States.

Division (GID) at the Department of Justice to analyze the issue. J. Edgar Hoover, future director of the FBI, was chief of the GID. By the fall of 1919, his group had concluded that these radicals were a serious threat to national security.

Palmer knew that he could use the loophole of wartime legalities to do things normally not allowed by the U.S. Constitution. Palmer instigated a series of raids throughout 30 U.S. cities. Unannounced, members of the Justice Department, along with local police, entered homes and businesses in search of immigrants. During the Palmer Raids, thousands of people were arrested, usually without a proper warrant. People were held for as long as four months without a trial. There was no evidence of any wrongdoing on their parts. The majority of these people were eventually released. However, 249 were deported because of the country in which they were born. Although the Palmer Raids were motivated by political discrimination, they show that, historically, U.S. public officials have let gross generalizations about groups of people determine their actions.

A "National Mistake"

The Palmer Raids are not the only example of extreme measures taken during times of war. Twenty years later, the bombing of Pearl Harbor horrified Americans. The Japanese bomber planes arrived early in the morning on December 7, 1941, without any warning. Within minutes, U.S. battleships were sinking and others were damaged. A great number of ships and combat planes were destroyed and more than 2,000 Americans died.

The country was in shock. But that shock quickly turned to anger and a passion for retaliation against

Japan. Suddenly, even those who had opposed being part of World War II were ready for the United States to become actively involved. While this was an understandable reaction, it led in a direction that has become known as one of the nation's most humiliating actions.

Driven by patriotic intensity, Americans began to look at all Japanese with suspicion. This attitude made its way to Congress, and many representatives wanted to deport any Japanese living in the United States. Congressman John Rankin of Mississippi stated during a session in Congress on February 18, 1942,

> *Do not forget that once a Japanese always a Japanese. I say it is of vital importance that we get rid of every Japanese whether in Hawaii or on the mainland. They violate every sacred promise, every canon of honor and decency. This was evidenced in their diplomacy and in their bombing of Hawaii. These Japs who had been there for generations were making signs, if you please, guiding the Japanese planes to the objects of their iniquity in order that they might destroy our naval vessels, murder our soldiers and sailors, and blow to pieces the helpless women and children of Hawaii. Damn them! Let us get rid of them now![3]*

Behind the Fences

Mary Tsukamoto, one of the people in a Japanese internment camp, stated, "We saw all these people behind the fence, looking out, hanging onto the wire, and looking out because they were anxious to know who was coming in. But I will never forget the shocking feeling that human beings were behind this fence like animals [crying]. And we were going to also lose our freedom and walk inside of that gate and find ourselves . . . cooped up there . . . when the gates were shut, we knew that we had lost something that was very precious; that we were no longer free."[5]

Even though many people tried to counteract this emotional swelling against the Japanese, few listened. A report about second-generation Japanese American citizens stated that almost all of them were loyal to the United States. This report, named the Munson Report, was written in October and November of 1941, before the Pearl Harbor attack.

The report did not make a difference in swaying public opinion. Finally, President Franklin Roosevelt signed Executive Order 9066, authorizing the military to set up designated areas and remove anyone they considered to be a national security threat. The order stated,

I hereby authorize and direct the Secretary of War . . . to prescribe military areas in such places and of such extent as he or the appropriate Military Commander may determine, from which . . . the right of any person to enter, remain in, or leave shall be subject to whatever restrictions the Secretary of War or the appropriate Military Commander may determine.[4]

The military immediately began evicting anyone with Japanese ancestry out of their homes throughout the Northwest. More than 120,000 Japanese living in the states of Washington, Oregon, California, Arizona, and Alaska were forced out of their homes. However, in the Hawaiian territory, people with Japanese ancestry were not deported. The islands depended on these people, and their absence would have upset the economic balance. Along the West Coast, however, Japanese were put in relocation centers that had been hastily built at racetracks and fairgrounds. From there, they were put on trains to American internment camps located in New Mexico, North Dakota, Texas, Montana, and other Western states. These camps were overcrowded and often did not have adequate supplies for everyone.

More than 70 percent of these internees had been born in the United States and were U.S. citizens. However, being of Japanese descent was enough to make a person a

The Internment Camp Facts

A total of 120,313 people of Japanese heritage were placed under the War Relocation Authority. Of those, 1,862 died during imprisonment.

After the camps closed:
• 54,127 returned to the West Coast.
• 52,798 moved into the central United States.
• 4,724 moved or were moved to Japan.
• 3,121 were sent to INS internment camps.
• 2,355 joined the Armed Forces.
• 1,322 were sent to institutions.

national enemy. Behavior did not matter. Heritage and race were their only crimes.

In 1976, on the thirty-fourth anniversary of Roosevelt's Executive Order 9066, President Gerald Ford publicly announced that the forced evacuation of the Japanese people was truly a "national mistake." Twelve years later, President Ronald Reagan signed HR 442, the Civil Liberties Act, to provide $1.65 billion in reparations for those Japanese internees still living.

The forced incarceration of the Japanese was truly one of American history's clearest examples of racial profiling. It was an example that would be referred to often in the years to come when the issue flared again.

Letters to a Librarian

Clara Estelle Breed was the Children's Librarian at the San Diego Public Library from 1929 through 1945. When many of the Japanese American children she had come to know were to be shipped to camps, she quickly handed out as many stamped and addressed postcards to them as she could. She asked the children to write to her and tell her what the camps were like. Today, more than 250 of these letters still exist and are on display at the Japanese American National Museum.

*People of Japanese descent arrive at an internment camp
in Washington in 1942.*

The September 11, 2001, terrorist attacks had a profound impact on the issue of racial profiling.

A New Kind of War

The morning of September 11, 2001, was sunny in New York City. People were going about their usual routines. The blue skies overhead were cloudless, crossed only by an occasional white jet stream or the silver glint of an airplane.

At 8:46 a.m., the view of the sky changed. An airplane was flying far too low. Seconds later, it crashed into the north face of the World Trade Center's North Tower. At 9:03 a.m., a second plane flew through the sky and hit the south face of the South Tower. Two other flights not far away also crashed, one into the Pentagon at 9:45 a.m. and another into a field in Pennsylvania at 10:10 a.m. This last plane was intended to reach either the White House or the U.S. Capitol Building.

From that moment, New York City would never be the same. Images of the destruction were played on television moments after they occurred. The nation was in shock. The state and country would never be the same. Broadcasters and newspapers used terms such as *jihad*, *al-Qaeda*, and *Taliban* in conjunction with Arabic names. National security became a huge issue. The problem of racial profiling would also never be quite the same as the focus shifted to Arabs—and anyone who happened to look remotely like an Arab.

From the President

A month after the events of 9/11, President George W. Bush addressed the nation: "Time is passing. Yet, for the United States of America, there will be no forgetting September 11th. We will remember every rescuer who died in honor. We will remember every family that lives with grief. We will remember the fire and ash . . . the last phone calls . . . the funerals of the children."[1]

THE WAR ON TERROR

In the terrorist attacks that came to be known as 9/11, almost 3,000 people were killed in a matter of hours. Most victims were in the World Trade Center towers, and there were no survivors in any of the airplanes. People were killed on the ground below the World Trade Center. Hundreds of police officers, paramedics, and firefighters also died as they attempted to rescue people inside the collapsing buildings.

The country was in shock from this act of terrorism, and the U.S. government scrambled to determine its response. The blame for this horrendous attack belonged to a Muslim terrorist group called al-Qaeda, led by a man named Osama bin Laden. Nineteen al-Qaeda members had been on those four planes. Fifteen of them were from Saudi Arabia, two were from the United Arab Emirates, one was from Egypt, and one was from Lebanon. Those 19 faces were shown all over the world on television stations and in newspapers. It was not long before many people looked at these men in much the same way that many Americans had viewed the Japanese 60 years earlier—with fear and loathing.

Daily reports of incidents of discrimination and hate crimes against Muslims, whether of Middle Eastern descent or not, began to soar. Mosques were attacked and even burned. People were angry and frightened. Racial stereotyping was rampant as people judged others as guilty simply for their race or religion.

Newspapers across the country printed editorials for and against the racial profiling of Middle Eastern people. Some argued against it passionately. They questioned whether racial profiling would result in

The 19 Men

In his book *Perfect Soldiers*, author Terry McDermott gives detailed descriptions of the 19 men responsible for carrying out the 9/11 attacks. He conducted months of research and interviews to discover the stories and backgrounds of the 19 terrorists.

He was surprised to find that most of the men did not come from military backgrounds. They came from middle-class families. At least one had spent a significant amount of time living in the United States. Not all of the men were overtly religious or particularly political. Many of them were described as polite, courteous, and friendly. McDermott found that, in most cases, the men were drawn to the idea of radical Islam and jihad—holy war—because they wanted to fight for a cause.

With Osama bin Laden, they were given the opportunity to fight against those whom their religion saw as corrupt. One investigator said that the 19 men became completely obsessed with their religion. They were well trained and taught specifically to fight against flight crews, which was exactly their mission.

McDermott also investigated al-Qaeda. He speculates that the organization is much smaller than many imagine. Its small size is what makes the group able to stay hidden.

Khalid Shaikh Mohammed is believed to be the organizer of the 9/11 attacks. He was captured in Pakistan in 2003.

unexpected complications. For example, terrorist organizations could recognize that the United States is focusing on certain types of people and begin recruiting people from groups that are not profiled.

Angela J. Davis, Professor of Law at American University's Washington College of Law, stated,

> *It is likely that anyone capable of orchestrating four simultaneous and deadly hijackings will be able to get around racial profiling. . . . Racial profiling invites a dangerous complacency.* [2]

Writers K. Jack Riley and Greg Ridgeway agreed in an article in Washingtonpost.com's *Think Tank Town.* They said,

> *We'd be naïve to think that terrorists won't follow the example of drug dealers and change their methods to circumvent a profile. Terrorists have, in fact, been doing this for years. To enter Israel for terror attacks, Hamas suicide bombers have disguised themselves as Israeli soldiers, Hasidic Jews and elderly people. Arab terrorists have dyed their hair blond to look like German tourists, and are known to be recruiting women, older people and converts to Islam to join terrorist ranks.* [3]

Suicide Bomber Profile

The Center for Human Rights and Global Justice at the New York University of Law claims that a suicide bomber profile does exist. The indicators may be:

- *the wearing of loose or bulky clothing in the summer;*
- *pacing back and forth;*
- *fidgeting with something beneath one's clothing;*
- *failure to make eye contact;*
- *being in a drug-induced state;*
- *strange hair coloring;*
- *wearing too much cologne;*
- *wearing talcum powder; and*
- *being overly protective of one's baggage.* [4]

The group also states that these vague indicators leave far too much room for error to be relied on fully.

Others applauded racial profiling in the light of the unified ethnicity of the 19 terrorists. Paul Sperry from Stanford University, for example, wrote in the *New York Times*, "Young Muslim men attacked New York with planes in 2001. From everything we know about the terrorists who may be taking aim at our transportation system, they are most likely to be young Muslim men." Perry goes on to say that profiling is "based on statistics. Insurance companies profile policyholders based on probability of risk. That's just smart business. Likewise, profiling passengers based on proven security risk is just smart law enforcement."[5]

Former New York City Commissioner Howard Safir agrees:

> We know that the 19 (9/11) hijackers were Middle-Eastern men between 18 and 23. . . . We know that the people who hit the Cole [a U.S. Navy ship] were the same profile. We know that the people who hit the embassies in Africa were the same profile. So, not using what we know—that the probability that a Middle-Eastern male between 18 and 23 is going to be a terrorist—not using that, is folly. And I think we should use it. But it's not racial profiling, it's terrorist profiling.[6]

In Times of War

In 2003, Jewish World Review columnist Stanley Crouch, an African American, wrote,

> *There is now the idea that we should just let as many people in from the Islamic world as ever because otherwise we're profiling Arabs. My attitude is that this doesn't apply during a war. People couldn't immigrate from Japan or Italy or Germany during World War II. That's a norm. It should be very difficult for anyone from the Islamic world to come into the U.S. The immigrant tradition in America cannot be applied whenever it means that we have to take the risk of letting in 19 men like those who hijacked the planes that achieved the greatest coordinated murder raid in world history.*

Never Forget

Brian Darling is a director at the Heritage Foundation, a research and educational institute based in Washington DC. He believes that common sense, such as watching for suspicious behavior, should be utilized in airport security. Some people think that race should not be considered when choosing who to screen; Brian Darling thinks these politically correct actions are incredibly dangerous.

Will innocent, moderate Muslims suffer because of this? Probably; most people suffer in some way when a war is being waged. Will we lose money if we make it very difficult to immigrate or enter this nation from Islamic countries? We already are. Billions. . . .

An Unexpected Terrorist

Not all terrorists are Muslim. Timothy McVeigh is an example of a non-Muslim terrorist. McVeigh was born in Pendleton, New York, on April 23, 1968. As a student, he often joined groups but soon quit, finding few friends. As a young man, he lived like a survivalist by hoarding food and firearms. At 20, he joined the U.S. Army. He attempted to qualify for Special Forces but could not meet the physical requirements. He was present in Waco, Texas, during the standoff between federal agents and the Branch Davidians, a religious sect.

Two years later, on April 19, 1995, McVeigh planted a bomb at the Alfred P. Murrah Federal Building in Oklahoma City, Oklahoma, killing 168 people, including a number of children. He was sentenced to death and executed in prison on June 11, 2001.

These are grim realities of our moment, and we run great and unnecessary risks if we are not willing to protect ourselves. Otherwise, it seems to me, that those who were burned alive, jumped from windows or were crushed to death Sept. 11, 2001, left this world in vain.[7]

In the wake of the 9/11 attack, racial profiling became a heated debate. Many Americans were unnerved by the fact that national security could be breached in such a calculated manner. Some declared that personal freedoms must be upheld, even in times of war. Others favored the use of profiling for the good of national security. The War on Terror caused many to rethink their views on racial profiling as the focus transitioned to al-Qaeda.

*Many Muslims living in the United States felt shunned after 9/11.
Some were eager to prove their loyalty to the United States.*

President George W. Bush signed the Patriot Act on October 26, 2001.

THE GOVERNMENT
RESPONDS

The government responded swiftly to the events of 9/11 and the growing unrest throughout the nation. Six weeks after the attack on the towers, President George W. Bush signed the USA Patriot Act into law. The law provides law enforcement with more authority in fighting terrorism. Bush stated,

> *The law allows our intelligence and law enforcement officials to continue to share information. It allows them to continue to use tools against terrorists that they used against . . . drug dealers and other criminals. It will improve our nation's security while we safeguard the civil liberties of our people. The legislation strengthens the Justice Department so it can better detect and disrupt terrorist threats. And the bill gives law enforcement new tools to combat threats to our citizens from international terrorists to local drug dealers.* [1]

Those who favor the Patriot Act say that it is a necessary step to ensure the safety, life, and liberties of American civilians. Those who oppose it say that it is a gross violation of personal freedoms and privacy. After it was signed into law, changes on the national, state, and local law enforcement levels were put into place to help find those responsible for the 9/11 attack and punish them, and to increase protection for the people of America.

INCREASING AIRPORT SECURITY

Airport security was not a new concept. In 1968, the Federal Aviation Administration (FAA) had formed the Federal Air Marshal program to reduce the number of hijackings to Cuba. In 1985, two Muslims tried to divert TWA Flight 847 to Beirut, Lebanon. After that hijacking, President Ronald Reagan directed the Secretary of Transportation to expand the program to cover international flights. Later that year, Congress passed Public Law 9983, the International Security and Development Cooperation Act.

After the attacks of 9/11, airports began a radical

The Patriot Act

H.R. 3162 is known as the USA Patriot Act. President George W. Bush signed it into law on October 26, 2001. The letters stand for "Uniting and Strengthening America by Providing Appropriate Tools Required to Intercept and Obstruct Terrorism Act."

This bill, created in response to the tragedies of 9/11, made many changes to how federal crimes were processed in the United States. It expanded the authority of U.S. law enforcement agencies in order to fight terrorism, including giving them the right to search telephone and e-mail communications as well as look through personal, medical, and financial records. This enabled the government to easily obtain wiretaps and other surveillance equipment in order to get evidence from sources such as Internet service providers and phone companies. It also gave them broader permission to share their findings with other federal agencies. Additionally, the Patriot Act allowed the U.S. attorney general to hold aliens or foreign individuals who are perceived as threats to national security for at least seven days without making any official charges.

Within days of this bill being passed, it had become a topic of controversy. Many people felt that the bill was a greater threat to people's privacy than it was to terrorist plots.

revamping of their security policies and equipment. The FAA was one of the agencies that changed a great deal after al-Qaeda's attacks. Before 9/11, there were approximately 50 federal air marshals in the program. After 9/11, President Bush signed another transportation safety law that expanded the funding for the program. This created the Transportation Security Administration (TSA) and jobs for as many as 2,000 air marshals. These officers can carry firearms and have the authority to make an arrest without a warrant based on a "reasonable belief" that a person is committing a federal felony offense. Although the presence of these air marshals has many potential benefits, the quality of the officers' training and education has been questioned.

Air Marshals

TSA says that on average, a federal air marshal spends five hours in an aircraft per day, flies 15 days per month, and flies 180 days per year.

DETAINING MIDDLE EASTERN MEN

After 9/11, the Department of Justice also began quietly gathering up Middle Eastern noncitizens to find a link between them and the terrorist events. More than 1,200 men were detained even though

CAPPS and the Secure Flight Program

In 1994, a program called Computer Assisted Passenger Pre-screening Systems (CAPPS) was developed. It helped airport security check passengers and carry-on baggage for dangerous items through the use of a computer. By 1998, most U.S. air carriers were using the system. After 9/11, the newly formed U.S. Department of Homeland Security developed CAPPS II. It required passengers to provide personal information when making reservations. Since then, that program has been replaced with the Secure Flight Program, which requires airlines to share the names of all passengers so that the government can compare each one with their master list of terrorist names.

they were not charged with any wrongdoings. It was the first large-scale detention of people based only on their country of origin since the Japanese internment camps of the 1940s. Federal agents entered Arab, Muslim, and South Asian communities and forced men to come with them. These men were taken from their homes, businesses, and mosques, usually without any explanation to them or their families. They were not allowed to call attorneys, seek counsel, or post bail.

These men were questioned for weeks and even months. Many of them were held in unsanitary, overcrowded environments. Many were verbally and physically abused by some of the federal correctional staff. They were not released until they were cleared of any possible links to al-Qaeda or other terrorist organizations. Not a single person detained by the government

Federal air marshals are trained at the Federal Law Enforcement Training Center in Artesia, New Mexico.

demonstrated any link to the terrorists and their actions against the United States. No charges were brought against any of these people.

VIOLATING PERSONAL FREEDOMS

As early as October 17, 2001, the ACLU began an official investigation into the government's immigrant detention. They sent letters to the U.S. attorney general, but did not receive a reply. They received no replies to the letters they sent to FBI

Testing the Security Systems

Nathaniel Heatwole wanted to see how effective airport security was. He planted box cutters, bleach, matches, and modeling clay (to resemble plastic explosives) on several Southwest Airlines jetliners. Then, he e-mailed TSA and told them where they could find the items. An FBI affidavit stated, "The email author . . . stated that he was aware that his actions were against the law . . . and that his actions were 'an act of civil disobedience with the aim of improving public safety for the air-traveling public.'"[2] U.S. Attorney Thomas DiBiagio replied, "It was not a test. It was not civil action. It was not public service. It was a very foolish and very dangerous course of action. . . ."[3] How was Heatwole able to smuggle these items onto the planes? He simply did not fit the terrorist profile.

Director Robert Mueller. The ACLU did not give up, however. They filed petitions and lawsuits and continue to fight for the rights of these detainees. In February 2008, the ACLU filed a lawsuit charging high-ranking government officials with depriving these Muslim, Arab, and South Asian men of their constitutional rights. It alleged that some of these detainees were constantly kept in solitary confinement in bright lights, deprived of sleep, forced to be nude, and not allowed any contact with their family or friends.

Attorneys for the Center for Constitutional Rights agreed with the ACLU. "John Ashcroft and other government officials have been trying to avoid accountability for the mass and indiscriminate round-up of innocent men after 9/11 for too long," says lawyer Michael Winger. "As architects of a plan to deprive these individuals of their rights, the blame for what happened to these men is squarely on their shoulders."[4]

Rachel Meeropol is the granddaughter of Julius and Ethel Rosenberg. The Rosenbergs were executed in 1953 after being convicted of conspiracy to commit espionage. About the situation, Meeropol stated,

> *Immigration law cannot be used as a short-cut around the Fourth Amendment. . . . Just because the executive wants to investigate a non-citizen, doesn't mean high-level officials can ignore the law. This should be made even more clear by the abuse our clients suffered while they were deprived of access to friends, family or counsel.*[5]

It is clear that the issues surrounding racial profiling in times of war are complicated. Proponents of racial profiling after 9/11 declare that this is a necessary step to keep a similar occurrence from happening.

An Important Memo

Just a matter of weeks before the events of 9/11, Phoenix FBI agent Kenneth Williams sent a memo to his superiors to investigate a number of Muslim men whom he suspected might be taking classes in U.S. flight schools. He believed they might be a part of a terrorist group. FBI director Robert Mueller did not see the memo. It was not sent to the CIA. According to an article in the *Los Angeles Times*, one of the men suspected in the memo was in contact with the hijacker who crashed a plane into the Pentagon. After 9/11, the Senate Judiciary Committee held private hearings to discuss how the memo fell through the cracks.

Opponents reject racial profiling and use examples of the violations of personal freedoms as their justification.

After the 9/11 attacks, Attorney General John Ashcroft warned terrorists that the U.S. government would take steps to put them in jail.

Osama bin Laden is a wealthy and secretive man.
He was born in 1957 in Saudi Arabia.

A NECESSARY EVIL

Many of the issues faced by the United
States today have clear sides, and there
are people who have strong stances for and against
an issue. Each side has spokespeople, educational

material, and political backing. This is not the case with racial profiling. Because opponents of racial profiling connect the issue with racism, vocal proponents of racial profiling can be difficult to find. Combined with the racist actions in U.S. history, racial profiling is a touchy subject.

SPEAKING OUT

In times of peace, there are few who vocally support racial profiling. Many fear that if they spoke up in favor of the practice, they would be labeled a racist. Opponents declare that those who favor racial profiling by default do not believe in racial equality or protecting civil rights. Some people might lose the trust and respect of others if they publicly supported racial profiling. For some, this could mean a loss of funding or support.

This attitude may be the reason no one reads about racial profiling

Necessary Steps?

Muslim American Oubai Mohammad Shahbandar has an interesting perspective on the issue of racial profiling post-9/11. Shahbandar stated, "Without life, there can be no liberty and pursuit of happiness. I pray the government will continue to take all steps necessary to safeguard us all. Mr. President, profile the terrorists."[1]

studies being done at universities. It is the reason that it is not argued in political debates. Anyone coming out in favor of profiling could be ousted. Today's culture is one that favors political correctness, tolerance, and acceptance. Speaking out in favor of racial profiling could be very offensive to some people.

UNUSUAL CIRCUMSTANCES

As history has suggested, the issue becomes debatable during times of war. When a nation is at war, an animosity can develop that results in bitter instances of racism, prejudice, and stereotyping. Sometimes these racist thoughts can lead to government-sanctioned actions, such as the setting up of internment camps for Japanese civilians during World War II. But are the racially motivated steps taken by the government in the name of protecting its citizens in times of war always wrong?

Certain Infringement

Michelle Malkin is an author in favor of racial profiling. Malkin recently stated in an interview, "One of the themes of my book is that civil liberties are not sacrosanct. While we should never be contemptuous of civil liberties, we ought not make a fetish of them either. When we are at war, certain infringements (e.g., military tribunals for suspected al Qaeda operatives), while regrettable, are justified."[2]

Many have taken on the topic of racial profiling during times of war in the safer arenas of magazine columns, newspaper editorials, and opinion pieces. These people have tried to state the facts and show why they believe racial profiling is a logical method for capturing potential criminals.

One of the first points supporters of racial profiling make is that everyone engages in profiling to some extent. For example, men are always profiled first when there is a serial killer at large. Why? Because statistically, men commit far more

A Final Word

Selwyn Duke is a columnist and public speaker. His work appears in conservative magazines as well as on Mike Savage's and Rush Limbaugh's shows. Duke believes that executing good profiling is common sense. He believes that law enforcement officers must be allowed to take all variables into consideration when they do their jobs. This includes using racially based profiles. Duke writes,

We now live in an age of terrorism and the knowledge that we're confronted with this grave threat should make it obvious that we don't have the luxury of doing a politically-correct dance-of-death around the issues. Much lip service is paid to how seriously we're taking security matters, to the Patriot Act, to this or that bill or that safety measure. But it all means nothing, absolutely nothing, unless we unshackle our minds and peer beyond the parameters established by the thought police. Unfortunately, one great failing of man is that he's loath to act until something jars him from his lethargy. In a time when that "something" could be a nuclear device that incinerates an American city, this failing is one that we indulge at our own peril.[3]

Senator George V. Voinovich discusses radical Islam in America during a Senate hearing about national security in January 2007.

crimes than women, especially murder. No one points this out as profiling. As columnist Selwyn Duke writes,

> *Let's say you walk down the street and see a pack of rough-hewn young men walking toward you and, quite prudently,*

you walk to the other side. Well, guess what? You've just engaged in profiling. Based upon the appearance of the individuals, your common-sense informed you that the probability was high that they posed a danger and you acted based upon that assessment. [4]

While politicians scramble to put together bills that protect the country and yet try to maintain people's civil rights, others disagree with this direction. Some say they have good reason to want to shine the spotlight on Muslims today because the facts show that the biggest danger is coming from this group of people. Those who favor racial profiling argue that even though the 19 terrorists on the 9/11 planes were from different places, they were all Arab and they were all Muslim. As an analogy, those who agree with profiling use the example of what happens in doctor's offices around the world. African Americans are prone to certain specific health conditions. When a doctor makes a special point of testing for those conditions, that is another example of using race and ethnicity to create a profile.

AROUND THE WORLD

Since 9/11, Islamic fundamentalists have attacked in Algeria, Jordan, Kuwait, India, Indonesia, Iraq,

Israel, Lebanon, Morocco, the
Netherlands, the Philippines, Russia,
Saudi Arabia, Spain, Thailand,
Tunisia, Turkey, and the United
Kingdom. Those who support
racial profiling say that we can use
information from past acts of terror
to prevent future terrorist attacks.
They think it is a bad idea to ignore
the facts about the types of people
who are committing these attacks.
Doing so is only aiding the terrorists
by letting them continue their
actions, they say. Jack Greer, a staff
writer for the *Stanford Review*, states,

> *Needless to say, most of the Islamic
> terrorists were Arabs. If the majority of
> those who seek to destroy us are Arabs,
> and if one of their traditional methods of
> attack has been to use airliners in some
> capacity (be it suicide or hostage taking),
> is there any good reason not to focus a
> certain degree of energy on this group of
> people?[5]*

Pinpointing Arabs

It can be very challenging to look at people and simply determine whether they are Arab, let alone Muslim. Of the 3 million Arabs currently in the United States, 63 percent of them were born in the United States. The largest group of Muslims in the United States is African American.

As far as respecting the civil rights of Arabs, John Derbyshire writes in the *National Review* that perhaps this country needs to "treat everyone with courtesy and apologize to the inconvenienced innocent."[6]

In Favor of Racial Profiling

Nationally syndicated talk show host Mike Gallagher is very direct when he talks about his belief that being politically correct puts every American at risk. In an interview in 2006, he stated,

> We have VIP lines at airport security checkpoints for first class passengers. We allow pilots and flight attendants to go to the head of the lines in order to make their flights on time. Let's extend that same convenience to Muslim passengers. After all, percentage-wise, there are fewer Arabs flying than non-Arabs, right? So it stands to reason that a Muslim-only security line would go quickly, even with

Limiting Luggage

As a possible solution, some people have suggested that the amount of carry-on luggage a passenger can bring onto a plane should be greatly limited. The thought is that the less a person can bring onto the plane, the less chance there is of a passenger smuggling an item that could be used for violence. However, there are concerns that limiting carry-on luggage would deter many from flying altogether and hurt the airline industry.

highly concentrated security efforts. Let's stop playing politically correct games and being worried about what the ACLU is going to do. This isn't some charade, this war is real. The terrorists who want to kill us are looking for every opportunity to pounce. It's time to formally and officially launch profiling in our nation's airports.[7]

While many people consider racial profiling wrong, no matter the instance, others see it in degrees. Post-9/11 profiling has been compared to the traffic stops made by police in various cities, but many experts point out that there is a huge difference between the importance of stopping a single car to check for drugs and stopping a mission of mass murder as with the hijackings. As Stuart Taylor Jr. writes, "[a] virulent perversion of Islam is the only mass movement in the world so committed to mass-murdering Americans that its fanatics are willing to kill themselves in the process."[8]

Even those who support racial profiling recognize that it can create awkward and unpleasant circumstances for people. But they consider it a necessary evil. Taylor writes,

Arab-Americans understandably resent being singled out and special scrutiny when boarding airliners. But the

alternative—a greater risk of being killed and greater political pressure for detention of relatives and other visitors from abroad who fall under unwarranted suspicion—are worse. [9]

An Inconvenient Burden

Those who see the benefits of racial profiling since 9/11 are often criticized for their frank opinions, but in the end, a number of people silently agree with them. Michelle Malkin, author of *In Defense of Internment: The Case for 'Racial Profiling' in World War II and the War on Terror*, states,

> *Post-9/11, the belief that racial, religious and nationality profiling is never justified has become a dangerous bugaboo. It is unfortunate that loyal Muslims or Arabs might be burdened because of terrorists who share their race, nationality or religion. But any inconvenience is preferable to suffering a second mass terrorist attack on American soil.* [10]

Some people will be embarrassed by being racially profiled. Innocent people will be targeted for suspicion because of the color of their skin and their appearance. People are going to continue to sue airlines and airports because of unfair treatment based on ethnicity. But for many who believe racial profiling has value, these inconveniences are

worth the risk. They believe that when it comes to protecting the lives of the thousands of people who board planes every day—regardless of nationality—the risk of hurting feelings and making a few mistakes is worth it.

Radio talk show host Mike Gallagher is outspoken about his beliefs that racial profiling in airports has benefits.

Anthony Romero is the executive director of the ACLU.

An Unnecessary Evil

Prior to the 9/11 attacks, the debate over racial profiling centered on local and state law enforcement agencies. Groups such as the ACLU argued against the use of racial profiling by police officers making everyday traffic stops and searches.

The ACLU claims that African Americans and Hispanics are more likely to be pulled over while driving than a white person, but no more likely to have drugs or weapons than a white person. The ACLU contends that this practice is widespread but highly ineffective, and needs to be stopped.

DENIES CIVIL LIBERTIES

Many believe that, prior to 9/11, the United States was close to completely condemning racial profiling in law enforcement. President George W. Bush had publicly criticized its use and many steps were being taken to end the practice. In 2001, prior to the terrorist attack, a national majority had vocalized a firm belief that racial profiling was unfair, uncivil, and unconstitutional.

Driving While Black

Before 9/11, it appeared that the focus of racial profiling in the United States centered on African Americans. A 2000 report emphasized this idea and created the term "driving while black." Many African Americans stated that they were being stopped by police officers for traffic violations more often than whites, Latinos, or other races. According to reports, African Americans are stopped, questioned, and searched even though they have not done anything wrong. Typically, police officers must have probable cause or a reasonable suspicion to search a vehicle, but there are some people who firmly believe that police officers consider being black enough to be suspicious.

But does that same argument apply during times of war? The ACLU and other groups say that it does.

Anthony Romero, the executive director of the ACLU, said,

> We saw the war on terror quickly become a war on immigrants. . . . A fair and open process is the only way to ensure that our law enforcement acts in accordance with our concern for civil liberties.[1]

The ACLU warns that interrogating and suspecting an entire religious community is ineffective in two ways: It does not effectively protect

The ACLU

The ACLU was founded in 1920. The ACLU is usually involved in controversial topics including abortion, the death penalty, civil rights, separation of church and state, illegal immigration, and racial profiling. It focuses on protecting the rights of Americans. As the group states,

> We work also to extend rights to segments of our population that have tradition-ally been denied their rights, including Native Americans and other people of color; lesbians, gay men, bisexuals and transgender people; women; mental health patients; prisoners; people with disabilities and the poor.[2]

Those who support the ACLU state that the organization is the nation's best "watchdog" in protecting the Constitution and people's basic rights. They look to the ACLU to be the country's defender of liberty.

Those who are against the ACLU believe that the group uses the court system to weaken the Constitution. They also think the ACLU does more harm than good.

The ACLU has more than 500,000 members and deals with more than 6,000 court cases every year. This includes an increasing number of racial profiling cases. Since 9/11, the group's membership has grown unusually quickly.

the nation from terrorists, and it does not protect the civil liberties of those suspected.

A VIOLATION OF TRUST

Opponents of racial profiling point out that the practice causes large rifts between communities and violates public trust in the government. They say that racial profiling causes resentment among those who are profiled and given a specific stereotype based on ethnicity. It also makes these targets less likely to cooperate in investigations. Opponents of racial profiling state that using preconceived notions and profiles is inaccurate and will not help deter terror.

The Leadership Conference on Civil Rights Education Fund authored *Wrong Then, Wrong Now: Racial Profiling Before & After September 11*. The report investigates the use of racial profiling in an age of terrorism:

"Research also has shown that a small proportion of high-risk offenders accounts for a large proportion of crime. An exhaustive study of career criminals conducted by the National Academy of Sciences found that while half of all offenders commit more than one crime per year, 10 percent of offenders committed over 100 crimes per year. A study in Baltimore found that almost 60 percent of adults arrested are on some type of criminal justice supervision (probation and parole) at the time of their arrest. . . . [I]t is clear that the majority of crime is committed by individuals who are not only well known to the law enforcement community, but who are also under criminal justice supervision."[3]

—*John D. Cohen, Janet Lennon, and Robert Wasserman,* Eliminating Racial Profiling: A Third Way Approach

These Muslim women protest the use of racial profiling against immigrants since 9/11.

Much of the support for post–September 11 profiling against Arabs, South Asians, Muslims, and Sikhs, is motivated by the confusion and anxiety that has gripped the nation since the terrorist attacks. . . . Terrorism profiling is a crude *substitute for behavior-based enforcement. It violates core American values, including the constitutional guarantee of equal protection. It also hinders anti-terrorism efforts because it alienates people and communities that are critical to the success of the anti-terrorism effort.* [4]

Opponents of racial profiling are quick to point out that it violates the civil rights of the individual. But if racial profiling is to be done away with, what methods should law enforcement and other governmental agencies use to track criminals and protect the U.S. public?

Other Options

Opponents say that if racial profiling is employed and used as the only measure to prevent terrorism, potential terrorists will find ways around the system. Instead, opponents propose the use of random searches. Doing this

A Police Resolution

The International Association of Chiefs of Police is the largest and oldest nonprofit organization of police in the world. In 2000, the Highway Safety Committee authored an article that stated their position on racial profiling. The group supports reasonable suspicion, not racial profiling, in traffic stops.

creates an unstable and unpredictable environment that could potentially deter terrorists.

Another option opponents suggest is the use of behavioral profiling. Proper training and the education of law enforcement officers, especially those in airports, could be a useful tool, in conjunction with thorough random searches and modern detection technology. Researchers and psychologists have studied the human behaviors connected with lies and deceit for years. One professor, Paul Ekman, researched how facial muscles related to human emotions. He continues to study how deception can be detected by studying the demeanor of a person.

The goal of using behavioral profiling is to train officers to detect the signs of nervousness, stress, disorientation, or deceit that could catch a potential criminal trying to conceal the truth. TSA began a trial

Racial Discrimination

The Convention on the Elimination of All Forms of Racial Discrimination was adopted by the United Nations in December 1965 and put into force in 1969. The resolution outlines the agreement that the deprivation of human rights and freedoms is wrong; therefore, racial profiling should be eliminated. A committee of elected officials meets twice a year for three weeks in Geneva. It reviews state complaints of racial profiling, as well as complaints from individuals.

of the technique in December of 2005 in more than ten airports. Employees were trained as "behavior detection officers." The system is still being tested, and although it could be useful, not everyone is confident in its effectiveness.

TECHNOLOGICAL OPTIONS

Other options include the use of current technologies. By relying on the large information databases kept by law enforcement agencies, officers should be able to make decisions based on accurate evidence, not merely physical appearance. Repeat offenders can be "flagged" in a system. Officers can focus their time on situations and people who credibly merit their attention. Advances in technology make the acquiring and spreading of information possible. This also suggests the possibility of a technological method of crime prevention based on legitimate evidence and not only physical appearance, although the two factors could be used together. Opponents of racial profiling suggest these options as alternatives to the practice of using racial profiles.

The terrorist attacks of 9/11 involved hijacked airplanes. It is clear that airport security is of the

highest importance in the United States and abroad. Opponents of the use of racial profiling in airports are eager to find a solution that maintains the safety of passengers and upholds the civil liberties that are protected by the U.S. Constitution. ⌐

People on both sides of the debate agree that airport security is a high priority.

Congressman John Conyers announces the End of Racial Profiling Act to reporters on June 6, 2001.

LEGISLATION REGARDING RACIAL PROFILING

As the tragedies and horrors of 9/11 began to fade from the headlines, pressure from groups such as the ACLU and Amnesty International kept racial profiling from fading into the background. President Bush and his cabinet were repeatedly reminded that racial profiling, as it was done before and after 9/11, violated a person's constitutional rights as put forth in the Fourth and Fourteenth Amendments. In early 2004, President Bush signed the End Racial Profiling Act, also known as the ERPA.

ERPA

The ERPA begins by listing the facts about racial profiling that Congress had accepted. It states,

A Look at Statistics

According to the ERPA, a Department of Justice report conducted in 1999 stated that "although African Americans and Hispanics were more likely to be stopped and searched, they were less likely to be in possession of contraband. On average, searches and seizures of African American drivers yielded evidence only 8% of the time, searches and seizures of Hispanic drivers yielded evidence only 10% of the time and searches and seizures of white drivers yielded evidence 17% of the time."[2]

Federal, State, and local law enforcement agents play a vital role in protecting the public from crime and protecting the Nation from terrorism. The vast majority of law enforcement agents nationwide discharge their duties professionally and without bias. The use of police officers of race, ethnicity, religion or national origin in deciding which persons should be subject to traffic stops, stops and frisks, questioning, searches and seizures is improper.[1]

The act points out how racial profiling is harmful to commerce because minorities may feel they are unable to travel freely. It also states that racial profiling is harmful to law enforcement because it undermines people's trust and confidence in the police force and its ability to protect citizens.

In reference to racial profiling and the Constitution, the bill states, "Using race, ethnicity, religion or national origin as a proxy for criminal suspicion violates the constitutional requirement that police and other government officials accord to all citizens the equal protection of the law."[3] The law states

Keeping Secure

In 2004, Screening Passengers by Observation Techniques (SPOT) was created. This program was designed to help airport security move away from racial profiling in their screening. It is based on watching for suspicious behavior rather than looking at a list of names or glancing at a person's appearance.

TSA's Federal Security Director George Naccara says, "This system is conducted by trained personnel and closely monitored by supervisors. It provides another significant layer of security."[4] TSA employees will watch for certain red flags in behavior such as anxiety, excessive sweating, odd mannerisms, or changes in the pitch of a person's voice. If such a person is identified, police may be called in for face-to-face interviews, and the person's name is also run against national criminal databases.

A report on SPOT in 2006 stated that to date, the program had caught more than 50 people with fake IDs trying to enter the country illegally or while possessing drugs. If it continues to be successful, SPOT will be part of all airports and possibly even other transportation systems such as trains and buses.

that it plans to enforce the constitutional right to (1) equal protection of the laws (Fourteenth Amendment), (2) protection against unreasonable searches and seizures (Fourth Amendment), and (3) interstate travel (Article IV of the Constitution).

The ERPA set up detailed directions on how to implement new programs, grants, and policies on the local, state, and national levels to stop racial profiling within the United States. It also laid out a national standard for data collection to track biased-based policing throughout the country. This was done to encourage police awareness and accountability. If police departments did not comply with this new ruling, the act allowed attorneys general to withhold department funds until they did.

The law effectively laid out the groundwork to stop racial profiling. But in 2007, the ACLU and other organizations were still working to get all of its proposed actions into place.

NSEERS

A year after the events of 9/11, the United States established the National Security Entry-Exit Registration System (NSEERS) program. It targets foreigners who currently live in the United States but were born in the following countries: Afghanistan, Algeria, Bahrain, Bangladesh, Egypt, Eritrea, Indonesia, Iran, Iraq, Jordan, Kuwait, Lebanon, Libya, Morocco, North Korea, Oman, Pakistan, Qatar, Saudi Arabia, Somalia, Sudan, Syria, Tunisia, United Arab Emirates, and Yemen.

The NSEERS program offers a way to track people of these countries if they entered or left the country. A year later, some of the requirements were changed and the organization continues to be a debated program.

*President Bill Clinton awarded Fred Korematsu
a Presidential Medal of Freedom in 1998.*

Fred Korematsu is one person who not only
has experienced racial profiling but is working to
fight against it. Korematsu was born in California
to Japanese immigrants. When President Roosevelt
issued Executive Order 9066 in 1942, he refused
to go to the internment camp. He was eventually
arrested and sent to the camp. But Korematsu

decided to bring a lawsuit against the United States for racial discrimination. After 39 years of court battles, a federal judge ruled in his favor. In 2003, Korematsu stated,

> There are Arab–Americans today who are going through what Japanese–Americans experienced years ago, and we can't let that happen again. I met someone years ago who had never heard about the roundup of Japanese–Americans. It's been 60 years since this [arrest] happened, and it's happening again, and that's why I continue to talk about what happened to me.[5]

While the initial rush of racial profiling that occurred after 9/11 has lessened somewhat over time, it continues to occur every single day in numerous places within the United States. Individuals and organizations committed to the protection of civil liberties continue to fight not only for legislation banning racial profiling, but also for the implementation of antiracial profiling laws that are already in place. The Leadership Conference

Sifting through Leads

Following the 9/11 attacks, the California Anti-Terrorism Information Center was founded. It was designed to analyze and process the thousands of tips and leads of suspicious terrorist activity that poured into various law enforcement agencies across the state. Using a secure, central database, professionals study the information carefully to determine if threats actually exist and, if they do exist, what approach to take. They constantly monitor multiple investigations using multiple agencies.

Attorney General

Almost six months after 9/11, Attorney General John Ashcroft stated, "This administration . . . has been opposed to racial profiling and has done more to indicate its opposition than ever in history. The President said it's wrong and we'll end it in America, and I subscribe to that. Using race . . . as a proxy for potential criminal behavior is unconstitutional, and it undermines law enforcement by undermining the confidence that people can have in law enforcement."[6]

on Civil Rights Education Fund offers a few suggestions for upholding the laws already passed. The group suggests disciplinary procedures for law enforcement officers who engage in racial profiling, as well as a complaint system for citizens who feel as if they have been treated unjustly. The group also advocates for funding to put these policies in place.

Passing a bill is not enough to change people's attitudes and perspectives, but bills can present a role model for people to follow. Opponents say that racial profiling as a practice is systematic and widespread, so the process of ending it will not be over soon.

This man protests the use of racial profiling in law enforcement.

The musician formerly known as Cat Stevens was removed from a plane from London to Washington in 2004. Stevens had converted to Islam and was on a security watch list.

Up Close and Personal

For many people in the United States, being judged or arrested based on skin color or ethnicity is not an issue they encounter on a daily basis. But for millions of others, it is a fact of life that they deal with frequently for themselves, their families, and their children.

The debate surrounding racial profiling is intensely personal. It deals with questions of national safety and individual freedoms. In many cases, the debate pits these two ideas against each other. Opponents of racial profiling give favor to individual freedom. Proponents of racial profiling for preventing terrorism declare that it is worth sacrificing individual freedom for greater safety. The issue questions what is most important.

> "The question is not whether Arab-looking people should be stopped, questioned, and searched based solely on their ethnicity. The question is whether airport security people should be allowed to consider ethnicity at all. The answer is yes, unless we are prepared to frisk everyone who seeks to board a plane, and until we have a security system so foolproof that we need not frisk anyone."[1]
>
> —*Stuart Taylor Jr.*

Freedom of Expression

In August 2006, a case involving racial profiling highlighted a possible violation of First Amendment rights to freedom of expression. Arabic architect and political analyst Raed Jarrar had gone through two airport checkpoints and was on his way to the boarding gate. He was approached by a TSA official identified as Inspector Harris. The inspector took Jarrar to the JetBlue Airways counter and quietly told him that he would have to remove his black T-shirt before getting on his flight. The shirt read,

"We will not be silent," in both English and Arabic. According to the TSA inspector, the Arabic script would make other passengers uncomfortable. "It is a dangerous and slippery slope when we allow our government to take away a person's rights because of his speech or ethnic background," stated Reginald Shuford, an attorney with the ACLU. "Racial profiling is illegal and ineffective and has no place in a democratic society."[2]

Jarrar's attorneys believe that Jarrar was clearly not a threat to security, but that his appearance alone made TSA officials single him out. His attorneys

From an Insider

Barbara Markham has been a police officer for more than 20 years, working primarily in undercover narcotics investigation. She has won awards and letters of commendation from the U.S. Department of Treasury–Bureau of Alcohol, Tobacco and Firearms for her work. In regard to narcotics and the racial profiling of African Americans, she told the ACLU in a telephone interview in 2003,

Racial profiling is utilized when you have no intelligence and you're just casting a wide net and having to use a process of elimination out of that wide net. Racial profiling is a lazy method for law enforcement. You're not using investigative skills; all you're doing is casting a wide net against one group, one segment of society, and that's what we call "going fishing" and you're going to come up empty-handed. The better way is to simply investigate terrorism by behaviors exhibited by specific individuals. It's not the color of one's skin or their ethnicity that should indict them or bring them under police scrutiny. It should be their behaviors or actions— what they do.[3]

also believe that the TSA officials decided upon the wrong course of action—instead of asking him to remove his T-shirt, they should have reminded the nervous passengers about the airport's safety regulations and reassured anyone who still felt uncomfortable.

Jarrar filed suit against the TSA official and JetBlue. Jarrar and his attorneys believe that the legal battle will help put an end to discrimination in airports based on appearance or speech.

THE OTHER SIDE OF THE DEBATE

Writer Stuart Taylor challenges readers to read a scenario to determine how they feel about racial profiling at airports:

> You are about to board a cross-country flight. Glancing around the departure lounge, you notice lots of white men and women; some black men and women; four young, casually

An Ineffective Waste

According to David A. Harris, an expert on racial profiling who testified before the U.S. Commission on Civil Rights, "As we embark in this new world, a world changed so drastically by the events of Sept. 11, we need to be conscious of some of the things that we have learned over the last few years in the ongoing racial profiling controversy. . . . All evidence indicates that profiling Arab Americans or Muslims would be an ineffective waste of law enforcement resources that would damage our intelligence efforts while it compromises basic civil liberties. If we want to do everything we can to secure our country, we have to be smart about the steps we take."[4]

dressed Latino-looking men; and three young, well-dressed Arab-looking men.

Would your next thought be, "I sure do hope that the people who let me through security without patting me down didn't violate Ashcroft's policy by frisking any of those three guys?" Or more like, "I hope somebody gave those three a good frisking to make sure they don't have box cutters?" If the former, perhaps you care less than I do about staying alive. If the latter, you favor racial profiling— at least of Arab-looking men boarding airliners.[5]

"There is one good reason why racial profiling should be acceptable: to help stop terrorists. Whether we like it or not, the United States is engaged in a global struggle against Islamic fundamentalists. Most of these terrorists hail from Arab countries. Therefore, it makes sense to pay special attention to those of Arab descent in order to deter and disrupt future terrorist attacks."[6]

—Jack Greer

Those who do not fit the terrorist profile do not always have to worry about the inconvenience or embarrassment of being detained based on how they look. But some Muslims who might fit the terrorist profile favor racial profiling. In 2006, Muslim Abdel Rahman al-Rashed, general manager of the al-Arabiya News Channel, wrote,

Writer and political commentator Anne Coulter has supported the use of racial profiling after 9/11.

It is a certain fact that not all Muslims are terrorists, but it is equally certain, and exceptionally painful, that almost all terrorists are Muslims. . . . We cannot clear our names unless we own up to the shameful fact that terrorism has become an Islamic enterprise—an almost exclusive monopoly, implemented by Muslim men and women.[7]

The issue of racial profiling in a post-9/11 world is a touchy subject for many. For those who stand up for civil liberties no matter what the circumstances, the issue is clear. But for those who believe that times of war call for desperate measures, the issue is a little cloudier.

These women hold photos of family members and friends who were killed in the 9/11 terrorist attacks.

*In-depth security checkpoints often mean longer
waiting times for flight passengers.*

WEIGHING THE
ARGUMENTS

*L*ike most of the controversies that exist
in today's culture, racial profiling
has advocates on each side. In an ideal world,
no one would be in favor of suspecting people

of wrongdoing based only on the color of their skin; in reality, that is almost impossible. The events of 9/11 radically changed the way the government, law enforcement officials, and civilians in the United States looked at the issue of racial profiling.

For those Middle Eastern people and Muslims who had nothing to do with 9/11 and are pointed at, attacked, ostracized, and interrogated, racial profiling is an injustice. It is unfair for these people to be grouped with terrorists with whom they have no connection. But for those who are trying to find ways to combat terrorism in the future, it seems to be a logical step to begin investigations among those people most like the 9/11 terrorists. Americans who grapple with the sorrow and tragedy of 9/11 may think that racial profiling is patriotic.

Synonymous?

Walter E. Williams, columnist for *Townhall.com*, wrote about racial profiling,

"A law-abiding Muslim who's given extra airport screening or a black who's stopped by the police is perfectly justified in being angry, but with whom should he be angry? I think a Muslim should be angry with those who've made terrorism and Muslim synonymous and blacks angry with those who've made blacks and crime synonymous."[1]

Opposed: Uphold Civil Liberties

Many people believe that enacting
federal laws and regulations to put an
end to racial profiling is a necessary
step on the part of the government.
These people point to the Bill of
Rights. They state that racial profiling
directly violates the personal
freedoms in the constitutional
amendments. However, they fear that
legislation is not enough to solve the
real problem. It is understood that
the problem is widespread and will
take a great deal of work to address.
There are loopholes in every bill and
unexpected side effects to every act.
In times of war, when the enemy has
a specific physical appearance, the
American people may meet that face
with fear and anger. They also know
that rules are not enough to change
the attitudes and perspectives of the
people. That takes examples, role
models, and most importantly, time.

"The terror attack on
the World Trade Center
and the Pentagon was a
tragedy for Americans. If
Muslims and other ethnic
and racial minorities are
profiled solely because
they belong to those
groups, this will only add
to the tragedy."[2]

—Mohamed Al-
Hamdani, Wright State
University

Earl Warren was a controversial Chief Justice. He was committed to racial equality and to fighting crime.

In 1999, Peter Siggins was appointed as the Chief Deputy Attorney General for Legal Affairs in the California Department of Justice. Siggins says,

> *Ethnicity alone is not enough. If ethnic profiling of middle eastern men is enough to warrant disparate treatment, we accept that all or most middle eastern men have a proclivity*

for terrorism, just as during World War II all resident Japanese had a proclivity for espionage.[3]

The Changing Face of Profiling

In David Harris's article "Flying while Arab" for *Civil Rights Journal*, he wrote,

September 11 dramatically recast the issue of racial profiling. Suddenly, racial profiling . . . became a vital tool to assure national security, especially in airports. The public discussion regarding the targets of profiling changed too—from African Americans, Latinos and other minorities suspected of domestic crime . . . to Arab Americans, Muslims and others of Middle Eastern origin, who looked like the suicidal hijackers of September 11. . . . The September 11 attacks had caused catastrophic damage and loss of life among innocent civilians; people were shocked, stunned and afraid. And they knew that all of the hijackers were Arab or Middle Eastern men carrying out the deadly threats of Osama bin Laden's al Qaeda terrorist network based in the Middle East, which of course claims Islam as its justification for the attacks and many others around the world. Therefore, many said it just makes sense to profile people who looked Arab, Muslim, or Middle Eastern. After all, "they" were the ones who'd carried out the attacks and continued to threaten us; ignoring these facts amounted to some kind of political correctness run amok in time of great danger.[4]

In Favor: Uphold National Security

Others believe that racial profiling during wartime is an unfortunate necessity. They believe that the political correctness of not wanting to cause anyone offense could ultimately end up costing Americans their lives. For the proponents of racial profiling during times of war, investigating those who hold similar beliefs and backgrounds as the 9/11 terrorists is a logical course of action. While they might agree that there are errors in the systems, they argue that racial profiling can be an effective tool in combating terrorism.

Michelle Malkin declares,

In the wake of 9/11, opponents of profiling have shifted away from arguing against it because it is "racist" and now claim that it endangers security because it is a drain on resources and damages relations with ethnic and religious minorities, thereby hampering intelligence-gathering. These assertions are cleverly fine-tuned to appeal to post-9/11 sensibilities, but they are unfounded and disingenuous. The fact that al-Qaeda is using some non-Arab recruits does not render profiling moot. As long as we have open borders, Osama bin Laden will continue to send Middle East terrorists here by land, sea and air. Profiling is just one discretionary investigative tool among many.[5]

Affirmative Action

Writer Michael Kinsley says that racial profiling is a great deal like affirmative action. Both practices pay particular attention to people based specifically on their race. The difference between the two practices is that affirmative action gives positive attention to a person, while racial profiling gives negative attention to a person. Ironically, people who are in favor of affirmative action tend to be against racial profiling.

The Challenge for the Government

U.S. history provides many examples of racially motivated actions executed during times when the nation was at war. Legislators have passed laws, such as the ERPA, to combat the use of racial profiling by ending its use among federal law enforcement agents. Today's government is charged with the task of how to avoid the mistakes of the past while not making a mistake that could end up costing lives.

Future Generations

Sherry F. Colb is a professor at Rutgers Law School in Newark, New Jersey. Regarding racial profiling, she said, "Whatever this nation decides, future generations may judge us as harshly as we now judge the supporters of internment during World War II. We must therefore consider our nation's past, present, and future in facing the difficult challenge of profiling in an age of terrorism."[6]

Racial profiling is a part of American culture and has been for centuries. As time has passed, the focus has shifted from one race to another. While the solution to racial profiling lies in encouraging unity, finding commonalities, looking below the surface, and eliminating crime, none of those are going to be easy to accomplish. ⌐

Airports try to maintain security without infringing upon personal freedoms.

TIMELINE

1669

The Commonwealth of Virginia passes the Casual Slave Killing Act.

1831

Whites retaliate for Nat Turner's Rebellion by killing more than 250 blacks.

1868

The Fourteenth Amendment is ratified.

1942

Executive Order 9066 is signed, authorizing the movement of Japanese to internment camps.

1965

The Convention on the Elimination of All Forms of Racial Discrimination is formed.

1968

The Federal Air Marshal program is developed.

1919	1920	1941
The Palmer Raids occur.	The American Civil Liberties Union is formed.	The Japanese attack Pearl Harbor on December 7.

1976	1994	1995
President Ford admits the internment camps were a "national mistake."	The Computer Assisted Passenger Pre-screening Systems program is developed.	Timothy McVeigh plants a bomb at the Murrah building in Oklahoma City.

TIMELINE

2001

Terrorists from al-
Qaeda attack the
World Trade Center
and two other sites on
September 11.

2001

President Bush signs
the USA Patriot Act
on October 26.

2004

The End Racial
Profiling Act is
created.

2004

Screening Passengers
by Observation
Techniques is
designed.

2002

The National Security Entry-Exit Registration System is developed.

2003

John Cerqueira is removed from an American Airlines flight on December 28.

2007

John Cerqueira is awarded $400,000 in the first legal victory in airline racial profiling post-9/11.

2008

The U.S. Court of Appeals vacates the decision of the lower court in favor of John Cerqueira. Cerqueira's attorneys petition for a rehearing.

ESSENTIAL FACTS

AT ISSUE

Opposed

❖ Racial profiling is a form of discrimination and violates rights provided for in the U.S. Constitution.

❖ Racial profiling is ineffective and terrorists will find ways to get around it.

❖ Personal freedoms are a higher priority than national security.

In Favor

❖ Racial profiling is terrorist profiling.

❖ The majority of terrorists are of Arab ethnicity, so it makes sense to focus time and attention on profiling similar people.

❖ National security is worth the risk of offending some people and making mistakes.

CRITICAL DATES

1942
Following the bombing of Pearl Harbor in 1941, President Roosevelt signed Executive Order 9066 and authorized the movement of Japanese to internment camps. People of Japanese descent were evicted out of their homes throughout the Northwest United States.

2001
Al-Qaeda terrorists attacked the World Trade Center on September 11. In the following weeks, President Bush signed the Patriot Act. Many Americans began to look at Muslims with fear and anger.

2002

The National Security Entry-Exit Registration System was developed. The program tracked people living in the United States who were born in specific Middle Eastern and African countries.

2004

The End Racial Profiling Act was created. The ERPA asserted that all forms of racial profiling in law enforcement are improper and that racial profiling undermines people's trust in police forces.

Quotes

"It should be remembered that practically all aliens have come to this country because they like our land and our institutions better than those from whence they came. They have attached themselves to the life of this country in a manner that they would hate to change and the vast majority of them will, if given a chance, remain the same good neighbors that they have been in the past regardless of what difficulties our nation may have with the country of their birth. History proves this to be true. . . . We must see to it that no race prejudices develop and that there are no petty persecutions of law-abiding people."—*Earl Warren, Fourteenth Chief Justice of the United States*

"If the majority of those who seek to destroy us are Arabs, and if one of their traditional methods of attack has been to use airliners in some capacity (be it suicide or hostage taking), is there any good reason not to focus a certain degree of energy on this group of people?"—*Jack Greer,* Stanford Review

ADDITIONAL RESOURCES

SELECT BIBLIOGRAPHY

Davis, Angela J. "Racial Profiling Post 9/11—Still a Bad Idea." *Brennan Center for Justice*. 19 Sept. 2008 <http://www.brennancenter. org/content/resource/racial_profiling_post_9_11_still_a_bad_idea>.

Harris, David. "Flying While Arab." *Civil Rights Journal*. Winter 2002. 19 Sept. 2008 <http://www.usccr.gov/pubs/crj/wint2002/wint02. pdf>. p. 6-13.

Hirschman, Kris. *Racial Profiling*. Farmington Hills, MI: Greenhaven Press, 2006.

Lobe, Jim. "Amnesty Intl.: Racial Profiling Much Worse Since 9/11." *Antiwar.com*. 14 Sept. 2004. 19 Sept. 2008 <http://www. antiwar.com/lobe/?articleid=3571>.

Willis, Anita L. "The Roots of Racial Profiling." *History News Network*. 23 Dec. 2002. 19 Sept. 2008 <http://hnn.us/articles/1167.html>.

FURTHER READING

Biddle, Wendy. *Immigrants' Rights after 9/11*. New York: Chelsea House Publications, 2008.

Halpin, Mikki. *It's Your World—If You Don't Like It, Change It: Activism for Teenagers*. New York: Simon Pulse, 2004.

Kops, Deborah. *Racial Profiling*. New York: Benchmark Books, 2006.

Marcovitz, Hal. *Race Relations*. Broomall, PA: Mason Crest Publishers, 2006.

WEB LINKS

To learn more about racial profiling, visit ABDO Publishing Company online at **www.abdopublishing.com**. Web sites about racial profiling are featured on our Book Links page. These links are routinely monitored and updated to provide the most current information available.

For More Information

For more information on this subject, contact or visit the following organizations.

American Civil Liberties Union (ACLU)
125 Broad Street, Eighteenth Floor, New York, NY 10004
212-549-2585
www.aclu.org
The American Civil Liberties Union is dedicated to the fight for individual rights. The ACLU serves to protect the civil liberties of all individuals, especially those groups that historically have been denied rights. The group handles nearly 6,000 court cases annually.

Center for Human Rights and Global Justice
110 West Third Street, Room 204, New York, NY 10012
212-998-6714
www.chrgj.org
The Center for Human Rights and Global Justice is affiliated with the New York University School of Law. The center focuses on legal research, especially in the area of the War on Terror.

National Archives Building
700 Pennsylvania Avenue Northwest, Washington, DC 20408
866-272-6272
www.archives.gov/dc-metro/washington
The National Archives Building displays the documents of United States freedom, including the U.S. Constitution and the Bill of Rights. The building also contains numerous documents and records for research purposes.

GLOSSARY

acquitted
　　To be found not guilty.

bugaboo
　　An imaginary object that causes fear.

civil liberties
　　Individual freedoms as provided for by the Bill of Rights.

demeanor
　　Behavior and outward manner.

deport
　　To expel from a country.

detain
　　To take and hold in custody.

espionage
　　Spying to gain knowledge about another government or nation.

fetish
　　An object that receives devotion, awe, or reverence.

fugitive
　　A person who flees or escapes.

hate crime
　　A crime that is committed intentionally toward a member or members of a specific racial, gender, or other group.

hijab
　　A Muslim head covering for women.

infringe
　　To violate the rights of another.

internment
　　The state of being captured or confined.

interrogate
　　To examine a person by questioning.

loophole
　　A means of escape or evasion, especially a way around a law.

lynching
> To put to death by hanging without legal cause.

mosque
> A Muslim house of worship.

petition
> A formally drawn request bearing the names of those making it and addressed to people in power asking for some right or benefit.

prejudice
> An opinion based on preconceived ideas instead of facts.

proclivity
> A tendency toward something.

racial profiling
> Suspecting a person of a crime based on race or ethnic background.

reparation
> Compensation or money that is given to make amends.

retaliation
> To get revenge.

sacrosanct
> Holy or treated as holy.

spontaneous
> Unplanned or random.

survivalist
> A person who makes preparations to survive a widespread catastrophe by storing food and weapons in a safe place.

systematic
> Regular, methodical.

vacate
> In legal terms, to vacate is to overrule or void a previous decision, sometimes because of error.

warrant
> A document certifying or authorizing something.

SOURCE NOTES

Chapter 1. At the Airport

1. "High-Flying Profiling: Portuguese-born US Citizen Wins First Legal Victory in Racial Profiling Case since 9/11." *Democracy Now!* 18 Jan. 2007. 22 July 2008 <www.democracynow.org/2007/1/18/high_flying_profiling_portuguese_born_us>.

2. Ibid.

3. Ibid.

4. "Victims' Accounts of Racial Profiling While Traveling through Airports." *Amnesty International USA.* 13 July 2008 <http://www.amnestyusa.org/racial_profiling/report/airport.html>.

5. S.2481. *The Library of Congress.* 11 Aug. 2008 <http://thomas.loc.gov/cgi-bin/query/D?c110:1:./temp/~c1105WeTyC::>.

6. "Ashcroft: Critics of New Terror Measures Undermine Effort." *CNN.com.* 7 Dec. 2001. 12 July 2008 <http://archives.cnn.com/2001/US/12/06/inv.ashcroft.hearing/>.

Chapter 2. A Look Back through History

1. Peter Siggins. "Racial Profiling in an Age of Terrorism." *Santa Clara University's Markkula Center for Applied Ethics.* 10 July 2008 <http://www.scu.edu/ethics/publications/ethicalperspectives/profiling.html>.

2. "U.S. Constitution: Fourteenth Amendment." *Findlaw.* 11 Aug. 2008 <http://caselaw.lp.findlaw.com/data/constitution/amendment14/>.

3. "Overview." *University of Washington Library.* 20 July 2008 <http://www.lib.washington.edu/exhibits/harmony/exhibit/intro.html>.

4. Ibid.

5. "Life in a WWII Japanese American Internment Camp." *National Museum of American History.* 15 July 2008 <http://americanhistory.si.edu/ourstoryinhistory/tryathome/activities_internment_more.html>.

Chapter 3. A New Kind of War

1. "Statement by H.E. Mr. George W. Bush." *UN.org.* 11 Aug. 2008 <http://www.un.org/webcast/ga/56/statements/011110usaE.htm>.

2. Angela Davis. "Racial Profiling Post 9/11—Still a Bad Idea." *Brennan Center for Justice.* 20 July 2008 <http://www.brennancenter.org/content/resource/racial_profiling_post_9_11_still_a_bad_idea>.

3. K. Jack Riley and Greg Ridgeway. "Racial Profiling Won't Stop Terror." *Washingtonpost.com.* 11 Oct. 2006. 25 July 2008 <www.rand.org/commentary/101106WP.html>.

4. "Irreversible Consequences: Racial Profiling and Lethal Force in the 'War on Terror.'" *Center for Human Rights and Global Justice.* May 2006. 11 Aug. 2008 <http://www.chrgj.org/docs/CHRGJ%20Irreversible%20Consequences.pdf>.

5. Paul Sperry. "When the Profile Fits the Crime." *New York Times*. 28 July 2005. 22 July 2008 <www.nytimes.com/2005/07/28/opinion/28sperry .html>.

6. Erick Stakelbeck. "Terrorist Profiling and Political Correctness: A Bad Mix." *CBN.com*. 24 July 2008 <http://www.cbn.com/cbnnews/ news/050826b.aspx>.

7. Stanley Crouch. "Will we allow those who were burned alive, jumped from windows or crushed to death on September 11, 2001, to have left this world in vain?" *Jewish World Review*. 11 Sept. 2003. 19 July 2008 <www .jewishworldreview.com/cols/crouch091103.asp>.

Chapter 4. The Government Responds

1. "USA Patriot Act." *whitehouse.gov*. 6 Aug. 2008 <http://www.whitehouse .gov/infocus/patriotact/>.

2. "Student charged in airline box cutter scare." *CNN.com/Law Center*. 21 Oct. 2003. 24 July 2008 <http://www.cnn.com/2003/LAW/10/20/ airline.scare/index.html>.

3. Ibid.

4. Jen Nessel. "CCR Challenges Racial Profiling of Muslim, Arab, South Asian Men in Post-9/11 Immigrant Detention Case at Court of Appeals." *Center for Constitutional Rights*. 24 July 2008 <www.commondreams.org/ cgi-bin/newsprint.cgi?file=/news2008/0214-16.htm>.

5. Ibid.

Chapter 5. A Necessary Evil

1. Oubai Mohammad Shahbandar. "I'm an Arab; Profile Me." *FrontPageMag.com*. 4 July 2003. 15 Dec. 2008 <http://www.frontpagemag. com/Articles/Read.aspx?GUID=AA8DD515-FA68-4796-ACB4- AA676C25DA0B>.

2. Jamie Glazov. "Malkin's Defense of Internment." *FrontPageMag.com*. 8 Sept. 2004. 4 Aug. 2008 <http://frontpagemag.com/Articles/Read .aspx?GUID=1EDCC47A-24E7-4839-8FF7-B6F90A2B4427>.

3. Selwyn Duke. "Time for less defiling and more racial-profiling." *Renew America.com*. 14 Jan. 2005. 30 July 2008 <www.renewamerica.us/ columns/duke/050114>.

4. Ibid.

5. Jack Greer. "Racial Profiling: Necessary Evil? Pro." *Stanford Review*. 25 Feb. 2005. 30 July 2008 <www.stanfordreview.org/Archive/Volume_ XXXIV/Issue_1/Opinions/ Opinions3.shtml>.

6. Ibid.

7. Mike Gallagher. "Politically correct airport screening puts us all at risk." *Townhall.com*. 18 Aug. 2006. 30 July 2008 <http://townhall.com/

Source Notes Continued

columnists/MikeGallagher/2006/08/18/politically_correct_airport_
screening_puts_us_at_risk>.
8. Stuart Taylor Jr. "The Case for Using Racial Profiling at Airports." *The Atlantic*. 25 Sep. 2001. 11 Aug. 2008 <http://www.theatlantic.com/politics/ nj/taylor2001-09-25.htm>.
9. Ibid.
10. Michelle Malkin. "Racial profiling: A matter of survival." *USATODAY*. 16 Aug. 2004. 11 Aug 2008 <http://www.usatoday.com/news/opinion/ editorials/2004-08-16-racial-profiling_x.htm>.

Chapter 6. An Unnecessary Evil
1. "ACLU Warns of Resurrecting 'Voluntary' Interview Program; Arab and Muslim Communities Should Not be Targets of Racial Profiling." *ACLU*. 22 June 2004. 11 Aug. 2008 <http://www.aclu.org/safefree/ general/18456prs20040622.html>.
2. "About Us." *ACLU*. 27 Aug. 2008 <http://www.aclu.org/about/>.
3. John D. Cohen, Janet Lennon, and Robert Wasserman. "Eliminating Racial Profiling: A Third Way Approach." *Progressive Policy Institute*. 15 Feb. 2000. 11 July 2008 <http://www.ppionline.org/ppi_ci.cfm?knlgAreaID=1 19&subsecID=156&contentID=610>.
4. "Wrong Then, Wrong Now: Racial Profiling Before & After September 11." *CivilRights.org*. 11 Aug. 2008 <http://www.civilrights.org/publications/ reports/racial_profiling/racial_profiling_report.pdf>.

Chapter 7. Legislation Regarding Racial Profiling
1. S. 2132. *Open Society Policy Center*. 24 July 2008 <http://www .opensocietypolicycenter.org/pub/doc_47/S.%202132%20End%20 Racial%20Profiling%20Act.pdf>.
2. Ibid.
3. Ibid.
4. Sally Donnelly. "A New Tack for Airport Screening: Behave Yourself." *Time*. 17 May 2006. 14 July 2008 <http://www.time.com/time/nation/ article/0,8599,1195330,00.html>.
5. Eric Paul Fournier. "Of Civil Wrongs and Rights: The Fred Korematsu Story." *PBS.org*. 19 July 2008 http://www.pbs.org/pov/pov2001/ ofcivilwrongsandrights/storyline.html.
6. "Fact Sheet: Racial Profiling." *Department of Justice*. 17 June 2003. 22 July 2008 <http://www.usdoj.gov/opa/pr/2003/June/racial_profiling_fact_ sheet.pdf>.

Chapter 8. Up Close and Personal

1. Stuart Taylor Jr. "The Case for Using Racial Profiling at Airports." *The Atlantic.* 25 Sept. 2001. 11 Aug. 2008 <http://www.theatlantic.com/politics/nj/taylor2001-09-25.htm>.

2. "ACLU Sues TSA Official, JetBlue for Discriminating against Passenger Wearing Arabic T-Shirt." *ACLU.* 9 Aug. 2007. 24 July 2008 <www.aclu.org/racialjustice/racialprofiling/34811prs20070809.html>.

3. Jim Lobe. "Racial Profiling Both Wrong and Counter-Productive, Says Amnesty." *CommonDreams.org.* 14 Sept. 2004. 11 Aug. 2008 <http://www.commondreams.org/headlines04/0914-03.htm>.

4. Zool Suleman. "Racial Profiling: Racism in Practice?" *Stop Racial Profiling.* 21 Mar. 2005. 24 July 2008 <http://www.cba.org/cba/newsletters/pdf/racial.pdf>.

5. Stuart Taylor Jr. "The Case for Using Racial Profiling at Airports." *The Atlantic.* 25 Sept. 2001. 11 Aug. 2008 <http://www.theatlantic.com/politics/nj/taylor2001-09-25.htm>.

6. Jack Greer. "Racial Profiling: Necessary Evil? Pro." *Stanford Review.* 25 Feb. 2005. 30 July 2008 <www.stanfordreview.org/Archive/Volume_XXXIV/Issue_1/Opinions/ Opinions3.shtml>.

7. Kathleen Parker. "Do Profile, Don't Tell." *Townhall.com.* 16 Aug. 2006. 24 July 2008 <http://findarticles.com/p/articles/mi_qn4176/is_20060817/ai_n16666876>.

Chapter 9. Weighing the Arguments

1. Walter E William. "Racial Profiling." *Townhall.com.* 20 Dec. 2006. 25 July 2008 <http://www.townhall.com/columnists/WalterEWilliams/2006/12/20/racial_profiling>.

2. Mohamed Al-Hamdani. "Racial Profiling." *The Guardian.* 16 Apr. 2003. 11 Aug 2008 <http://media.www.theguardianonline.com/media/storage/paper373/news/2003/04/16/Opinions/Racial.Profiling-419183.shtml>.

3. Peter Siggins. "Racial Profiling in an Age of Terrorism." *Santa Clara University's Markkula Center for Applied Ethics.* 10 July 2008 <http://www.scu.edu/ethics/publications/ethicalperspectives/profiling.html>.

4. David Harris. "Flying While Arab." *Civil Rights Journal.* Winter 2002. 26 July 2008 <http://www.usccr.gov/pubs/crj/wint2002/wint02.pdf>. 7.

5. Michelle Malkin. "Racial profiling: A matter of survival." *USATODAY.* 16 Aug. 2004. 11 Aug 2008 <http://www.usatoday.com/news/opinion/editorials/2004-08-16-racial-profiling_x.htm>.

6. Sherry F. Colb. "The New Face of Racial Profiling: How Terrorism Affects the Debate." *FindLaw.* 10 Oct. 2001. 11 Aug. 2008 <http://writ.news.findlaw.com/colb/20011010.html>.

INDEX

ABOUT THE AUTHOR

Tamra Orr is the author of more than 150 nonfiction books for people of all ages. She lives in the Pacific Northwest with her four children, husband, dog, and cat.

PHOTO CREDITS

David McNew/Getty Images, cover; LM Otero/AP Images, 6; Kathy Willens/AP Images, 13; John Zich/Corbis, 17, 88; William Henry Shelton/Corbis, 18; Washington Clinedinst/Library of Congress, 23; Paul Wagner/AP Images, 29; Chao Soi Cheong/AP Images, 30; Khalid Shaikh Mohammed/AP Images, 34; Timothy A. Clary/AFP/Getty Images, 39; Doug Mills/AP Images, 40; J. R. Hernandez/AP Images, 45; Rick Bowmer/AP Images, 49; AP Images, 50, 80, 91; Joe Raedle/Getty Images, 54; Buzz Orr/AP Images, 61; George Nikitin/AP Images, 62; Spencer Platt/Getty Images, 66; Douglas C. Pizac/AP Images, 71; Evan Vucci/AP Images, 72; Dennis Cook/AP Images, 76; Daniel Hulshizer/AP Images, 79; Rachel Denny Clow/AP Images, 85; Susan Walsh/AP Images, 87; Charles Rex Arbogast/AP Images, 95